Professor Richards Coaching & Consulting Books

How to Fix Mistakes 101

From the…

Professor Richards 101 Book Series

Dr. Soyini Richards has a bachelor's degree in Sociology and Psychology, a Master's degree in Counseling Psychology and a PhD in Business Psychology. She followed her mother's footsteps and entered the field of education after completing her first degree. Dr. Richards fell in love with psychology and education early during her tenure as an undergraduate student at Howard University.

Professor Richards is a serial entrepreneur who has dedicated her life to celebrating, educating and empowering others. She lives in the Washington, DC area, and is a native New Yorker who also lived for almost a decade in the suburbs of Atlanta, Georgia.

How to Fix Mistakes 101

From the…
Professor Richards 101 Book Series

Dr. Soyini Ayanna Richards

Professor Richards Coaching & Consulting

How to Fix Mistakes by Soyini Richards, Ph.D. Published by Professor Richards Consulting

www.ProfessorRichards.org

For permissions contact: info@DrSoyini.com

ISBN: 978-0-578-24932-2

Printed in the Unites States of America

This Book is Dedicated to . . .

...my grandmother, Minna Theresa Brooks, the most influential human being in my life who encouraged me to seek the Lord with all my heart.

...my daughter, Gabrielle Ayanna, in whom I am well pleased.

...my parents who have always believed in me and wanted the best for me.

…my mother, Barbara Richards, who I finally understood when it was too late after she went home to our Lord.

…my father, Hugh Richards, my hero.

...my little sister, Anika, and little brother, Joel, who are very dear to me.

...my grandchildren who I love like no other and will forever strive to help give them the best.

...last and certainly not least, my circle (you know who you are).

Table of Contents

Preface

This book is part of my series of self-help instructional books called Professor Richards 101 Series. *How to Fix Mistakes 101* explores the concept of *mistake* and unveils the possibilities behind the use of the word.

Ultimately, I pose the question, what is a mistake? I go beyond the basic dictionary definition and present alternative options on a road to fixing mistakes. Mistakes, errors, regrets, and related challenges are explored to find meaning in our story.

I yearned, cried, begged God so many times for a do-ever, second chance, or an eraser. He probably laughed, cried, and wished I would stop. I stopped. I'm writing this book to help others stop too.

Today, I live free of regrets and free from condemnation. After years of travailing through my thoughts of what if's, I finally came to a place of all is well. I have learned how to understand this journey called life and make sense of the parts of the journey that don't make sense.

We are not on this journey alone. I developed the theories to "fixing mistakes" on Biblical principles, wise quotes, my experiences, others' experiences, hidden truths, cultural awareness, song lyrics, and hope.

MISTAKE

mis·take | \ mə-ˈstāk \
mistook\ -ˈstu̇k \; **mistaken**\ -ˈstā-kən \; **mistaking**

verb

transitive verb

1: to blunder in the choice of
//*mistook* her way in the dark

2a: to misunderstand the meaning or intention of **:** MISINTERPRET //don't *mistake* me, I mean exactly what I said **b:** to make a wrong judgment of the character or ability of //The army's leaders *mistook* the strength of the enemy.

3: to identify wrongly**:** confuse with another // *I mistook* him for his brother

intransitive verb

1: to be wrong

Merriam-Webster

MISTAKE

mis·take | \ mə-ˈstāk \
mistook\ -ˈstu̇k \; **mistaken**\ -ˈstā-kən \; **mistaking**

noun

1: a wrong judgment - MISUNDERSTANDING **2:** a wrong action or statement proceeding from faulty judgment, inadequate knowledge, or inattention

Merriam-Webster

ERROR

er·ror | \ ˈer-ər , ˈe-rər \

noun

1a: an act or condition of ignorant or imprudent deviation from a code of behavior

b: an act involving an unintentional deviation from truth or accuracy made an *error* in adding up the bill

c: an act that through ignorance, deficiency, or accident departs from or fails to achieve what should be done // an *error* in judgment
: such as

(1): a defensive misplay other than a wild pitch or passed ball made by a baseball player when normal play would have resulted in an out or prevented an advance by a base runner

(2): the failure of a player (as in tennis) to make a successful return of a ball during play

d: a mistake in the proceedings of a court of record in matters of law or of fact

2a: the quality or state of erring the map is in *error*

b: an instance of false belief

3: something produced by mistake a typographical *error* *especially*: a postage stamp exhibiting a consistent flaw (such as a wrong color) in its manufacture

4a: the difference between an observed or calculated value and a true value *specifically*: variation in measurements, calculations, or observations of a quantity due to mistakes or to uncontrollable factors

b: the amount of deviation from a standard or specification

5: a deficiency or imperfection in structure or function an *error* of metabolism

Merriam-Webster

MISHAP

mis·take | \ mə-ˈstāk \
mistook\ -ˈstu̇k \; **mistaken**\ -ˈstā-kən \; **mistaking**
mis·hap | \ ˈmis-ˌhap, mis-ˈhap \

noun

1: an unfortunate accident. The fire was a tragic *mishap* that could have been prevented.

2: bad luck: Misfortune The ceremony proceeded without *mishap*.

Merriam-Webster

Introduction

I wrote this book on the premise that there is no such thing as a mistake. Whether you believe that the Bible is the uncompromised Word of God or not, this book will offer you peace, hope, and perspective on the concept referred to as a mistake. I present various Biblical principles, theories, and historic quotes. In addition, I share thoughts of resolution surrounding errors and mishaps. In each chapter, I develop my claims and unravel the sting and mystery of the word MISTAKE.

Also, I assert the idea there is no such thing as a coincidence. Furthermore, I examine the philosophy that nothing in life is a true accident, but part of a bigger picture.

I have made my share of so-called mistakes. I've gone down the wrong road. I have also trusted the wrong people. I used to live frustrated in a cloud of regrets. I can go on and on about the dismay. This history and experience led me down a path to discover how to make sense of this whirlwind. I discovered a light at the end of the tunnel.

This book will take you on a journey to make sense of what looks like a life of mistakes or wrong turns. Whether you believe in fate, believe you control your own destiny, or you don't have a position on the issue at all, this book will offer insight on the matter.

If you experience confusion around the concept of God's sovereign will, I will present an exploration of the endless possibilities. Each chapter approaches various dynamics we face in life pertaining to the outcomes of our decisions, paths, and situations.

After years of contemplation, living with regrets, and torturing myself over *what if's*, or *I should haves*, I learned it is important to know how to deal with this idea of "mistakes." I guide you through your thoughts to help you learn from errors and what to do when you may have missed the mark.

The information shared in *How to Fix Mistakes 101* promotes constructive thinking. This type of thinking allows one to think constructively about their world and environment. Constructive thinking fosters less of a reaction to events, but an opportunity to interpret before responding. Such thinking supports our growth and development while minimizing disruption with the external environment.

The suggestions offered in this book will help *free* you from bitterness, promote self-forgiveness, discourage unforgiveness, reduce fears, stomp hopelessness, eliminate self-condemnation, and rid you of despair. The right choices lead to the correct paths that carry you to good decisions.

Questions will be posed to help you ponder possibilities. The questions are to aid the shifting of your mindsight to believe and trust your Creator has a positive outcome for your life.

Would you like a life with no more regrets, and discover tools to "letting go"? If you believe in mistakes, it is a mistake to not allow yourself to live WHOLE. May you find peace after reading this book to carry through your chapters of life. Choose not to allow yourself to hurt anymore.

Chapter 1

Guess what?
You are Human &
People Make Mistakes

The English poet Alexander Pope said, "To err is Humane; to Forgive, Divine." The spelling of human as humane by Pope was not a mistake, but the use of the original spelling in the early 18th century.

Considering we are humans, we make what people call mistakes and errors. Are you consumed by a mistake or a wrong someone has done to you?

We must forgive ourselves, and others, when they make an error. In turn, others will forgive us. In addition, help yourself by helping others. In the book of Job, his well known story of trial and tribulation was turned around when he prayed for his friends.

Forgiving and forgetting is not always a package deal. It may be important to remember to safeguard oneself from further violation or pitfalls. Distancing oneself from offenders may be necessary to survive.

The key to is finding peace with a matter while moving forward. The late Colin Powell was a well accomplished American politician, statesman, diplomat, and the first African American Secretary of State. He is known for many leadership quotes. One quote is "Peace is an indicator of right action." An ideal goal is to seek *right action*.

The story of the Prodigal Son reveals God comes running to you after one goes out on their own to do things their way. The loving Father God welcomes his children back with open arms when they return to him after running through the wilderness.

Run to your loving, kind, merciful Father God for help and everything you need. God is the good shepherd and will look for all His lost sheep to guide them. He is our shepherd who leads us to the right path. Read Psalm 23 in the King James version written by King David.

The LORD is my shepherd; I shall not want. He maketh me to lie down in green pastures: he leadeth me beside the still waters. He restoreth my soul: he leadeth me in the paths of righteousness for his name's sake. Yea, though I walk through the valley of the shadow of death, I will fear no evil: for thou art with me; thy rod and thy staff they comfort me. Thou preparest a table before me in the presence of mine enemies: thou anointest my head with oil; my cup runneth over. Surely goodness and mercy shall follow me all the days of my life: and I will dwell in the house of the LORD forever.

A question posed throughout history is do we have free will or is there a sovereign will of God. The mystery will go on, but can we agree the outcome is the priority?

Ultimately, fulfillment, satisfaction, and peace, is our goal. The Lord's grand design and vision for our lives began in our natural mother's womb according to what was written in the Bible's book of Jeremiah. Verse 5 in the first chapter spoke to the prophet and said…

Before I formed you in the womb
I knew you,
before you were born
I set you apart
before I formed you in the womb,
I knew you.
Before you were born,
I set you apart for my holy purpose.

Another's Path

Yes, we can learn from the mistakes of others, but everyone's path is unique. Proceed with caution when people in your circle are in your ear giving their two cents. They found their own way and didn't necessarily listen to the advice of others. If they did or didn't listen, their present situation doesn't ensure it is because of someone's advice. Furthermore, professional guidance from a therapist, coach, clergy, mentor, and advisor is provided with caution, as well as a disclaimer that unknown factors may impact results.

A word of warning: if multiple people are telling you the same thing about a person or situation, the warning may require further investigation and consideration. Take heed to the warning.

Maturity plays a natural role in how we make decisions. One's development, upbringing, environment, circumstances, and ability to make choices also impact day-to-day decisions.

Having a peace, following your gut feelings, and tapping into your inner knower are also tools to making decisions. Using those particular tools require "practice" and testing over time.

Knowing what tools to use is important. Each day we developing decision making skills. Sometimes it is necessary to use multiple tools and resources to navigate through choices.

Keep in mind that people are not "at their best" when they are hungry, tired, fearful, or sick. If you are experiences conditions that cause you not to be "yourself", it isn't the most ideal time to make decisions. If you are faced with no other choice, but to make a move seek assistance, support, and guidance. You don't have to proceed alone.

Decisions may need tweaking, adjustment, or further consideration. We may change our minds. Something may have been overlooked after gathering more details. Are those changes or adjustments mistakes?

All have considered alternate options to a decision, changed their mind, or pondered on possibilities other than the course previously taken. Pencils have erasers. Computer programs have undo commands like *control Z.* A computer keyboard has a backspace key. Painters use drop cloths. Streets have u-turns signs.

Fear of making mistakes could result in procrastination, carelessness, and more errors. No, this is not a pass to be sloppy or careless. Nor am I suggesting you have a pass to do harm to others or not express remorse for wrongdoing.

Things happen. Issues come up. Health, financial, family, society, cultural, marital, relationships, work, and a plethora of matters occur daily. Day to day we face life's issues.

"*Fear not*" is one of the most common commands in the Bible. The words "Fear not" is mentioned approximately 365 times in the Bible. Fear of making a mistake should not paralyze or hinder people from making decisions.

Do not fear errors or failure, but rather use them as feedback to bring you closer to successful outcomes. Fear can be crippling. Don't let fear hinder your future.

Life is a process. Errors are all a part of the process. The process is evolving, learning, and adapting. The process is meant to help you learn and grow.

Evolve	**Learn**	**Adapt**

When picking fruits and vegetables, the challenge is selecting the one with the least damage. Despite the rise of genetically modified food, food items are rarely perfect.

We discover the use of dinks, holes, and scrapes despite the inconvenience, pain, or discomfort. Discovering use in the middle of imperfection offers revelation, answers, and hope. There is too much stress surrounding striving for perfection. Perfection is an impossible standard.

Striving for excellence is not striving for perfection. Excellence is…

"Excellence is to do a common thing in an uncommon way." —Booker T. Washington

We are what we repeatedly do. Excellence, then, is not an act, but a habit." —Aristotle

"Excellence is not an exception; it is a prevailing attitude." —Colin Powell

The will to win, the desire to succeed, the urge to reach your full potential... these are the keys that will unlock the door to personal excellence." —Confucius

What is perfect? Who is perfect? What has no blemish that is living? Is there a possibility that what you think was a mistake is part of developing a unique experience?

Where do straight roads lead you? A curvy path will still lead you to your destination. It is actually a more interesting ride to go up hills, around corners, under bridges, over bridges, through the water, in the woods, sliding through mud, and hit a bump every once in a while.

Ride the road and wear your seat belt. You will survive. The most important thing is to arrive at your destination. How you get there isn't as relevant once you arrive.

For example, when you get off a plane that had a lot of turbulence, you often forget the scary experience once you begin your adventure and your destination. Furthermore, you more than likely will get on a plane again.

How do you cover all your tracks? Is it possible to cover all your tracks?

Is an error our knowledge failing us or our judgment failing us? There is a possibility both didn't work out the way we thought or work out ideally.

Is ignorance a blank sheet on which we may write our story? Is an error a scribble one forms that must be erased? Is learning how not to grieve over our errors the goal? Let's pause and ponder on these things.

Evaluating options is useful when we have the opportunity. Misunderstandings happen. Questions, feedback and comments may be a necessary element of the evaluation process.

Mistakes can be expected, inspected, and respected. Some mistakes are embarrassing, catastrophic, or even irredeemable. The reality is you can't undo some things or do something about everything. Looking back constructively is beneficial to navigate your future steps. It may be necessary to objectively look back to navigate your future without condemnation or finding fault.

The reality is you can't undo some things or do something about everything.

Finding peace with decisions is important. Prior to making decisions, it helps to ask yourself if you will be at peace with the decision?

Show me the way I should go Lord.

Psalm 143:8

Maxwell Martz is the author of *Psycho-Cybernetics* (1960). He lived from March 10, 1899 – April 7, 1975. His theory is a system of ideas that he claimed could improve one's self-image leading to a more successful and fulfilling life. Martz is known for the quote "You make mistakes. Mistakes don't make you."

Be careful not to enter a state of futility. When you are not motivated to try and think, it is difficult to try. That's experiencing futility. Don't take the path of hopelessness. It will lead you to believe that no matter how much you do, nothing good will happen, and you might as well give up. No! That is not an option. Have hope. Never give up, nor settle. Don't lose faith in your judgment.

God did not create us like Mister Geppetto, the fictional character in the 1882 novel *The Adventures of*

Pinocchio by Carlo Collodi. The character created the wooden puppet Pinocchio with strings. The character, Pinocchio, frequently gets into trouble and is often impulsive, as well as mischievous. God is not a puppet master. He is an endearing, loving, and tender Father.

God is not producing a tv show or a film like the *Truman Show* movie starring Jim Carrey. His character grew up in what he thought was an ordinary life, but unbeknownst to him, he was living on the set of a television show about him. The 1998 comedy-drama or dramady uniquely covered simulated reality, existentialism, surveillance, religion, metaphilosophy, privacy, and today's reality television.

Do you take comfort in knowing God created you and had a plan for you in your mother's womb according to Jeremiah 1:5? In addition, Ecclesiastes 3:11 says, *the Lord made everything beautiful in its time*. Also in chapter 3, verses 1 – 8 we are offered encouragement by recognizing there is a season and a time for every activity here on earth.

I remember my dear Grandma Brooks, who went home to see our Lord at 101 years old, referred to the word haste frequently. She would tell me haste and go do this or don't haste but take my time. She referred to haste as to rush and act speedily.

We must not haste when it comes to making all decisions, but haste to listen. In the Bible's book of James, and in chapter 1 verse 19, we are instructed *to be swift to hear, slow to speak, and slow to wrath.*

You are choosing your future by what you do now. There is a time for both birth and death. Also, there is a time to plant and a time to harvest. Recognize your time.

Hope	**Time**	**Reality**

Chapter 2
Decisions & Choices…
Mistakes & Errors

The Lord is your Shepherd.
Psalm 23:1

In Psalm 23, the Lord referred to Himself as our shepherd. Our Father knows we need his protection and guidance. This chapter in Psalms opens with we should lack nothing or want of anything. This implies, our Father, the Shepherd, provides what we need in life.

We are never alone because the Lord is by our side. Deuteronomy 31:6 in the New American Standard Version of the Bible instructs us to…

Be strong and courageous,
do not be afraid or
in dread of them,
for the LORD your God
is the One
who is going with you.
He will not desert you or abandon you.

This blessed assurance is to be reassuring. Things happen. Let's move on. I know it isn't as simple as it sounds. This thinking requires correctly right sizing the experience. Situations appear different in the moment. Stepping outside yourself and evaluating the circumstances requires understanding options.

What are the vantage points? The vantage point provides a full range of solutions. It offers a position or standpoint from which something is viewed or considered. Have you looked at the various point of views of the situation?

A diamond in the rough refers to someone or something whose good qualities are hidden. When a diamond is uncut, it does NOT look like the sparkling gemstone found in a ring.

A Potter's clay goes through great heat and transformation before the beautiful outcome. The clay becomes strong as it withstands heat and pressure. The pushing and molding form a foundation. Ultimately, the masterpiece is formed. A potter can make a "bad" piece of clay good.

Could it be that nothing happens to you, but for you?

The world is full of turnaround stories. God promises to make crooked places straight in our lives (Isaiah 45:2 KJV). He also promises to perfect that which concerns us (Psalm 138:8). There is no waste of time. Time, moments, and experiences matter. They make your story. They make the world's story. Could it be that nothing happens to you, but for you?

Some errors are unknown. Falling under deception may be observed a root cause or contributing factor of an error. One may eat or partake in a particular food item for years that was bad for them. One may live in a home with undetected toxic fumes as radon, or concealed mold. That may be considered a mistake. Not all *mistakes* are apparent.

One day you may have clarity on a matter. In fact, you may *lol* at the situation. Yes, laugh out loud. Therefore, it is important not to give certain circumstances the energy or too much emphasis. Avoid following a path that may bring you down, or trip you up. Yes, life may be long and sweet if we take the road of wise decisions, but opportunities to discover alternative paths may be adventurous and more interesting.

Decisions, decisions …choices, choices…there are so many of both. There are estimates that we make approximately 35,000 decisions a day. There are 86,400 seconds in one day. We are busy making decisions.

Decisions	**Judgment**	**Actions**

Throughout life, we are choosing between love and ambition, or emotions and being practical. Our motives, drives, and experiences can heavily impact our thoughts which ultimately impact our decisions.

Unfortunately, along our roads, there may be detours, speed bumps, construction, and traffic. Maps may be confusing, or navigation systems may fail us. The choice really is yours on how you drive on the road, or what resources you use and do not use along the way.

U-turns are not always an option. Sometimes stop signs are necessary to regroup recharge and learn a lesson. There are very few dead ends. Fortunately, there are more cul-de-sacs enabling us to turn around rather than dead ends requiring substantial maneuvering.

Decision-making is vital and necessary. Our entire existence hinges on the decisions we make. Decisions create tragedies or joy, laughter or tears, pain or pleasures. Although, don't let anyone or circumstances rush you into decisions before you are prepared. Be patient and proceed expeditiously when you can or absolutely necessary. Patience can be used as a tool to magnify deception and avoid pitfalls.

Patterns we model after and the tools we were provided all impact our future.

When evaluating decisions, it is helpful to evaluate what we observed along the way growing up. Patterns we model after and the tools we were provided all impact our future. Each experience helps catapult us further. It is important to navigate through our emotions to avoid making emotional decisions. Emotions may complicate and fog up our decision lenses.

As we analyze our journey, we benefit from making peace with the past. Unresolved pain can impede sound decisions. Exercise emotional intelligence. Various sources define emotional intelligence or emotional quotient (EQ) as the ability to understand, use, and manage your own emotions in positive ways to relieve stress, communicate effectively, empathize with others, overcome challenges and defuse conflict.

When solving a problem, or making a decision, choosing the appropriate approach is often the key to arriving at the best solution. Learning to how to make good a decision starts early. I remember guiding my daughter through the decision-making process when she was little. I would give her a choice for breakfast. I asked her if she wants waffles or cereal while reminding her that she had waffles the day before. I would say "You'll savor the flavor for waffles if you miss it for a day." She learned how to make decisions as she practiced making better and better choices deliberating over the options. The process gets easier and although more complex as life becomes more involved.

We make several decisions in an hour. Remember, 35,000 decisions a day? Some decisions are minor, and some are major requiring thought, strategy, or assistance. An individual's approach to the same choice may require different preparation. Counting the cost and balancing certainties against risks requires attention. Identifying short-term gratification against long-term benefits is another area of consideration.

Some decisions or choices may have clear right or wrong options, but likelihoods and possibilities that are uncertain remain an option even in the light of all available information. Decision-making can be complicated. It is often challenging to think objectively about all the variables, and often enough we just don't know all the odds of different possible outcomes. Sometimes we don't have time or are too emotional to think clearly or effectively.

Research on the topic of decision-making reveals people will generally use a quick, gut-level, unconscious, usually emotion-driven response that is rooted from personal experience. The research on the topic also describes another frequent approach as a slower, more deliberative, and analytical process that rationally evaluates available information to determine benefits versus costs.

It is important to review problem-solving strategies. Mistakes, decisions, and problems are all in the same family.

The concept and noun "margin of error" is defined by *Merriam Webster* as a measure or degree of difference. When the concept is referred to as a statistic it expresses the amount of random sampling error in the results of a survey. Consequently, the larger the margin of error, the less confidence the poll results would reflect the result of a survey of the entire population.

The term margin of error is often used in non-survey contexts to indicate observational in reporting measured quantities. It is also commonly used when referring to the amount of space or amount of flexibility one might have in accomplishing a goal. In sports and games margin of error describes how much precision is required to accomplish goals, points, or specific outcomes.

Ultimately, margin of error is usually a small amount that is allowed in case of miscalculation or change of circumstances. Life in general have these moments requiring contemplation.

Each semester in my General Psychology class, I review the topic: *Thinking, Problem-Solving and Cognition.* When introducing problem-solving, various approaches are introduced. One is Algorithm. An algorithm is a process or set of rules to be followed in calculations, or other problem-solving operations. This is a step-by-step procedure that solves logical and mathematical problems. Recipes are an example of an algorithm. The proper steps, ingredients, temperature, and timing all make the recipe come together.

Heuristic is another problem-solving strategy introduced. While an algorithm must be followed exactly to produce a correct result, the heuristic is a general problem-solving framework. Heuristics can be described as mental shortcuts utilized during making decisions as trial and error, a rule of thumb, or an educated guess.

Taking Shortcuts is not always an option. Real-world problems are often complicated. It may be tough to think objectively about all possible variables and determining what the odds of different outcomes may be a challenge. Our brains are naturally wired to reduce that complexity by using the mental shortcuts *of heuristics*. Researchers have identified numerous ways humans simplify decisions via heuristics and the potential bias such shortcut-thinking can produce.

Ultimately, when the problem-solving matter is initiated, perception is activated pertaining to the matter. Then, what follows is emotion, intellect, expression, and environment. Lastly, culture and experience also influence the matter. The problem-solving process relies on navigating through these areas.

At times a pros and cons list can help determine steps to take. I often share with my clients and students how writing things out to brainstorm or engaging in mind mapping activities can help you view things clearly. Processing details on paper while viewing possibilities and essential components can bring clarity to a matter.

Seeking revelation and insight during the decision-making process is part of our journey. Later, in chapter 5, we explore what is learned from so-called mistakes and the errors of life.

The Biblical reference to Jesus performing the miracle of turning water into wine is well known even by people who profess they don't "believe in the Bible". The story is found in the 2nd chapter of the book of John. Verse 5, tells us Jesus' mother said to the servants at the wedding, "Whatsoever He saith unto you, do it." The servants began to follow Jesus' instructions to serve the water without hesitation. The miracle came to pass, and the water was turned into wine.

Obedience to promptings and instructions from God requires faith. Did you really hear from God? What if it is God? What if you are wrong? What if you are right?

The questioning causes delay and the deliberation may require testing or stepping out on faith. It is important to identify if the incident is an opportunity for God to be glorified and for you to advance in His plan for your life is key.

The opportunity may be a life changing moment to bring you to a higher level. Each positive and "correct" move builds our confidence, as well as faith. Our spiritual ears are developed from stepping out on faith experiences.

The Biblical account of the woman with the issue of blood is found in the book of Luke and in chapter 8 versus 43-48. She suffered from hemorrhages for twelve years and spent all her resources on physicians with no positive results. The woman stepped out on faith and pressed forward to touch Jesus. Once she touched the hem of Jesus' garment, immediately her hemorrhaging stopped. The woman followed the prompting, acted in faith and received the desired results.

WORDS...

Our choice of words is important as is our perspective. Word choices and perspective can turn things around. How about putting a semi-colon in the middle of the sentence story and not a period? A semicolon is a punctuation mark (;) indicating a pause. It is typically between two main clauses and is more distinct than a comma.

Some people allow one decision that took them on the wrong path to continue to take them on several wrong paths spiraling them into a series of confusion and challenges to get back on track. There are moments, we need a semicolon to briefly pause, quickly regroup but continuc.

You can't focus on the future and the past at the same time. Focus on your desired future. The Bible says in Philippians 3:13, "forgetting what is behind and stretching toward what is ahead." The wonders and possibilities of the future is a gift.

The 1999 film starring the award-winning actor, Tom Hanks, *Cast Away,* told the story of a nearly catastrophic plane crash leaving him isolated on a remote island. Hank's character struggled to survive a journey on the will to survive. His character explored the blessings and heartache of fate, while demonstrating the strength of the human spirit. Tom Hans' performance led him to an Academy Awards nomination.

There was a touching scene in the movie after Hanks returns from years stranded on an island. He said to his love interest played by Helen Hunt he should never had gotten on that plane.

Yes, it was a movie, but their lives would have been a different story if those decisions were different. Tom Hanks said he was so sorry. The apology will never change anything in their story. This is an awesome example of how their decisions created paths leading them to lose each other, and to alternate realities. Watch the movie.

Furthermore, Tom Hanks' character shared with his friend the accounts of living on the island for 4 years alone. Hanks explained how he held onto the hope to live because he never knew what the tide would bring in. A tide brought in a sail that ultimately aided his return to civilization.

What will the tide bring you?

Chapter 3

Perspective:
Is it Really a Mistake?

Jesus once said, "You do not realize now what I am doing, but later you will understand."

John 13:7

Have you asked yourself, is it really a mistake? Is it really wrong? Was that really a coincidence?

Was that really a coincidence?

The unknown, chance, and possibilities all offer alternatives to a so-called mistake. If you change what you did, you wouldn't be who you are today? This is not necessarily suggesting you are what you do. Change your thinking and you change your life.

Is there a time, or do you feel in general missed or passed over? There's a wisdom that we don't know about right now. God's ways are not our ways according to John 13:7 from the New International Version (NIV). Who are we to question God?

Suffering is a part of living in a fallen world like Job whose popular story in the Bible reminds us it can happen for reasons we may never know about. He didn't know the conversation God had presented in the first chapter of the book of Job. God has a purpose for us that goes beyond the pain one endures. Don't get discouraged. Pray to our great physician, our Lord, to give us words to heal the pain.

When your vehicle has a recall, you go to the manufacturer for a modification or an update. We seek our Creator, our manufacturer, for repair and to put us back on the right track.

What you thought was a mistake may not be a mistake, but part of a plan, or bigger picture. The matter may have gotten your attention to cause you to check in with your Creator.

What you thought was a mistake may not be a mistake, but part of a plan, or bigger picture.

There is comfort in believing nothing in your life is an accident. Wrap your mind around that possibility. Yes, you could miss boats or a free opportunity if you are too late. What else could you have missed? Will you be more prepared next time you feel the same type of prompting? Each incident is a lesson and a step in the right direction as you move forward.

Pondering on the phenomena of coincidence, there may be experiences that made you scratch your head. Other incidents clearly look orchestrated, or intentional leading us to an unintended ending.

Coincidence is defined as a remarkable concurrence of events or circumstances without an apparent causal connection. Can this be? Some cultures and languages do not recognize or have a word for the concept coincidence. Does everything have a connection?

Decisions start with deciding what conclusions are to be made about a matter. How to handle decisions that didn't turn out the way you planned requires being open. Second-guessing ourselves will needlessly nag our hearts and confuse our thoughts.

You may not have avoided that accident if your phone didn't go dead preventing your alarm from waking you up. What did that delay save you from? What accident did we miss? What tragedy did we circumvent?

My dear sweet Grandma Brooks told me a story when I was growing up that left a lasting impression on me. She fell ill, which was a rare occurrence. Her mother had plans to attend an annual party on the train in their community. My great-grandmother was very disappointed because she had to stay home to take care of my grandmother.

The train had a terrible accident during the party. Many people lost their lives or limbs. People who survived the wreck endured major injuries or were paralyzed. My great-grandmother was not on the train. No that wasn't a mistake or coincidence. This is an example of how to have a new perspective of disappointments. The disappointment was for a good.

God loves us unconditionally. He sits alongside you with your pain not to watch you suffer, but to show you his love and how He can deliver you from all evil. The popular *Footprints* picture reflects this side-by-side relationship we have with our Lord. The picture highlights two pairs of footsteps in the sand.

God is our father, friend, confidant, deliverer, and so much more. God is what we need. In the book of Ezekiel in the Bible. There is a reference to God being our wheel in the middle of a middle wheel.

The reference demonstrates the enduring connectedness to the power from above. I once read "If you want to be sure it's the right destination, just walk with God." Let Him be your pilot.

It is also important to look at the gravity of a situation and right-size the severity.

Use new lenses. Things look clearer with microscopes, magnifying glasses, or eyeglasses. During eye doctor visits, we are given tests by looking through various lenses. It is also important to look at the gravity of a situation and right-size the severity.

Not everything that is faced can be changed. But nothing can be changed until it is faced.

James Baldwin

If you reverse some of your actions, you wouldn't have experienced some of the best things that happened to you. The most challenging trials or devastating relationships may result in the biggest rewards.

Ponder on a line from the song *Do What You Do* by Jermain Jackson of the legendary Jackson 5. "How can something so right go so wrong".

Relationships are a great example of how things are not always what they appear. A relationship, marriage, or partnership that did not turn out the way you expected isn't necessarily a mistake.

Who are we to question the process of seasons in our lives? Who are we to question if something was supposed to be or not be?

Like a mother who waits nine months to deliver her child, the pain she went through during delivery is not equal to the reward of the child. Children may be born into a relationship that don't work out, one-night stands, and even rape. Also, families are formed from adopting a child and blended families from previous relationships.

I will never forget knowing a mother who every other word was about her child. It was clear she was so proud to be a mother and found so much joy in the relationship. She shared with me one day that the child was conceived during a rape. I was amazed to discover this child she spoke of so endearingly was the result of such a violent and horrific act. That mother's love superseded the tragic beginning of her child's life.

I once read…

Forget the things that made you sad
and remember those that made you glad.
Forget the troubles that passed away
and remember the blessings
that come each day.

My Theoretical Framework pertaining to navigating through life positively is described in the graph and figure below. Be careful not to let the former years negatively impact the years you have ahead.

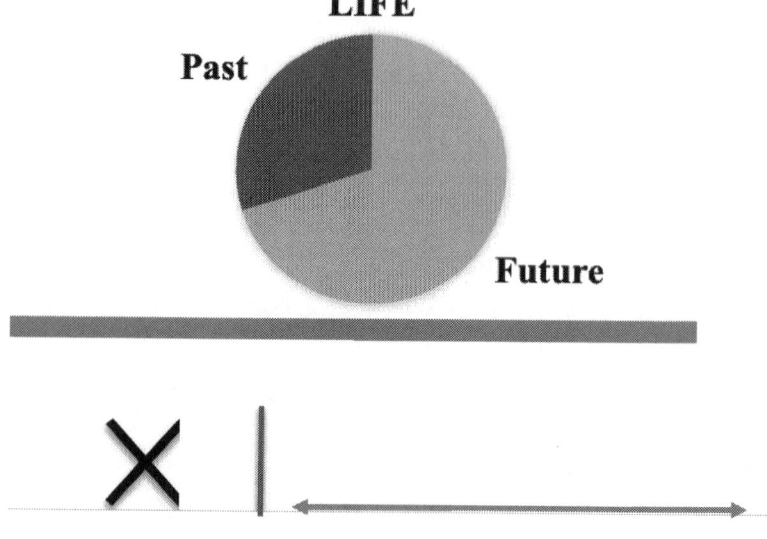

Can someone look at a life and say it was a mistake when they look at the possibilities in their existence? Whether they used those possibilities or made wise decisions, they left their mark on this earth.

Whether a previous experience was traumatic, or a confounding circumstance was life challenging, life goes on. Out of tragedies and loss, gifts and discoveries are made.

Can someone look at their life and say it was a mistake when they look at the possibilities in their existence?

Maybe a real hearty cry will help during one of those stop signs. A check-in with a therapist may help you recharge at a gas station. Also, pray without ceasing for energy to push you through. Get help to continue down the road so you can make it to your destination. Several resources are available to help along the way. You are not alone in this journey.

Yes, some matters are irreversible, but time heals. Lessons are learned through each experience. Let God be God in your life.

Choices are discussed in various chapters, and while discussing a variety of topics in this book, ask yourself tough questions like "why was that choice placed in my path"? "What did I learn"? "Would I be who I am today"?

The wonders of the world, mysteries of life, moles, birthmarks, and even birth defects are distinctions that make us different, as well as unique. These things identify us and set us apart from others. There are no human carbon copies. Even identical twins have differences.

Great creations were made from so-called errors.

Could it be the blunders, bloopers, and oops are part of a bigger plan or purpose? Great creations were made from so-called errors. Countless recipes, fashion, designs, and masterpieces came to pass unintentionally.

The following page provides an extensive list of accidental, unintentional, and oops inventions. Fascinating discoveries were made that changed the world. Some items may surprise you.

Accidental Inventions

Anti-Malarial Drug
Beer
Botox Treatment
Brandy
Bubble Wrap
Champagne
Cheese Curls
Chewing Gum
Chocolate Chip
Cookies Coca-Cola
Dippin' Dots
Dry Cleaning
Dynamite
Fireworks
Ice Cream Cone
Ice Cream Cones
Corn Flakes
Ink Jet Printers
LED Lighting
Matchsticks
Microwave Oven
Non-Stick Teflon
Pacemaker
Pap Smear
Penicillin
Play doh
Popsicles
Post-It Notes
Potato Chips
Saccharin *(The 1st Artificial Sweetener)*
Safety Glass
Scotchgard
Silly Putty
Slurpees
Stainless steel
Super Glue
Tea Bags
The Color Mauve
Safety Pin
Slinky
Tofu
Tonics
Vaseline
Velcro
Viagra
X-Rays
Yogurt

Life is full of hidden mysteries. Unveiling, revealing, and discovering is a part of the process while navigating through life.

Inventors have found there is a thin line between life-changing innovation and failure. Alexander Fleming discovered penicillin from a mishap. Wilson Greatbatch discovered the pacemaker by pulling the wrong device out of a box.

Inventors are known for creating inventions accidentally. An unknown cook in China is recognized for accidentally making a mixture that resulted in fireworks.

Household favorite foods like chocolate chip cookies, potato chips, ice cream cones, and corn flakes cereal were created by accident. Coca-Cola was also discovered while trying to create a tonic for headaches and hangovers.

Did you know x-rays were created from a "mistake?" Velcro and Viagra are other items invented by accident too. What would our world be without those mistakes? Your so-called mistake may be the next thing to change society.

Ivan Pavlov's famous dog study that revealed what we know about classical conditioning started out as research on digestion. The Russian physiologist did not intend to go down in history for embarking on groundbreaking psychology research.

Keeping all this in mind, it is still important to be aware of distractions and pitfalls that may take you off course. The Bible in *Proverbs 14:12* warns us of deception making people do something that appears right but may end up tragic. The circumstances of life can deceive people to turn and twist while making them think they are doing the right thing.

The worst thing that ever happened to you may be the best thing that ever happened to you.

Ponder on the possibility that the worst thing that ever happened to you may be the best thing that ever happened to you. Is it possible what you thought was wrong was actually right? Could being late actually mean you were on time? Could the act of forgetting to do something actually mean you shouldn't have done it? Ultimately, what is true, real, right, wrong, or supposed to be? Each day we learn live and learn to live in our truth.

A common phrase I quoted during the COVID-19 or also known as the corona virus pandemic was from a line in Charles Dickens' 1859 novel, A Tale of Two Cities. "It was the best of times; it was the wort of times". The following is the full opening text of the novel.

> *"It was the best of times, it was the worst of times, it was the age of wisdom, it was the age of foolishness, it was the epoch of belief, it was the epoch of incredulity, it was the season of Light, it was the season of Darkness, it was the spring of hope, it was the winter of despair, we had everything before us, we had nothing before us, we were all going direct to Heaven, we were all going direct the other way–in short, the period was so far like the present period, that some of its noisiest authorities insisted on its being received, for good or for evil, in the superlative degree of comparison only."*

This statement is listed among one of the most famous opening lines of a book. Ponder on that passage which is quite a long what could be called run on sentence.

Dickens is describing conflicts between wisdom and foliness, evil and good, light and darkness, as well as ups and downs. The book takes the reader through an array of strong emotions from intrigue, surprises, disappointments, and recovery from despair.

Some statements make you pause and wonder. *"To be, or not to be"* is one of the most widely known and quoted lines in modern English. It is a soliloquy that has been referenced in innumerable literary works, theatrical lines, and lyrics.

A soliloquy is an act of speaking one's thoughts aloud when by oneself or regardless of any hearers. A popular example of a soliloquy is from Romeo and Juliet when Juliet speaks her thoughts aloud when she learns that Romeo is the son of her family's enemy: O Romeo, Romeo!

"To be, or not to be" is the opening phrase of a soliloquy given by Prince Hamlet in William Shakespeare's play *Hamlet.* This is recognized to be one of the most thought-provoking quotes of all time.

In the scene, Hamlet is pondering on the pain and unfairness of life. He is contemplating death and suicide. Hamlet acknowledged that the alternative and unknown might be worse. The monologue presents the thoughts in the midst of an existential crisis.

This type of crisis refers to feelings that may lead to questioning the meaning of one's existence. Existential crisis may also present unease about life's meaning, choices, and freedoms.

Theorists in this area are called existentialist who consider an existential crisis a journey, an awareness, a necessary experience, and a complex phenomenon. Ultimately, it would be ideal for one experiencing such a crisis to find their Creator who can reveal their truth, be their savior and their answers.

This chapter wraps up with words from Oprah Winfrey shared during a Stanford Graduate School of Business interview. Ms. Winfrey encourages people to live out the truest highest expression of themselves and surrender to God's dream for their LIFE.

This guidance is aligned with God's plan of abundant life for us. The message is available on YouTube as "Take Care of Yourself Motivational Speech". Below are some bullets from the interview.

- There are no mistakes.
- You have a supreme destiny and calling. Feel and know that.
- If you are not listening, you get off track.
- You get as much from your losses as you do your victories.
- Failure is to point you into a different direction.
- Be still and ask yourself, what is the next right move?
- Your life is bigger than that one moment.

Chapter 4

Look for potential.
Is there a Ram in the Bush?

"You Make Your Mistakes to Learn How to Get to the Good Stuff"
~ Quincy Jones

To proclaim the favorable year of the LORD
and the day of vengeance of our God;
to comfort all who mourn,
to grant those who mourn *in* Zion,
Giving them a garland instead of ashes,
the oil of gladness instead of mourning,
the cloak of praise instead of a disheartened spirit.
So they will be called oaks of righteousness,
the planting of the LORD,
that He may be glorified.

Isaiah 61:2-3 New American Standard Bible

What did God save you from? Have you ever watched an artist draw a picture? During the early stages, it looks like a big mess. Consider the disarray, and what may look like chaos when building a house, baking a cake, or CREATING almost anything. During the initial process, only the Creator may hold the vision for the outcome.

Recognize the beauty in imperfection. Move grow learn and evolve taking each step. Like a toddler walking unstable but eyes focused on what's ahead.

Move	**Grow**	**Learn**	**Evolve**

We have a merciful God who wants to be our everything. Nothing is too bad, messed up, or too far gone for Him to handle. In fact, it appears He likes those big jobs so He can show off His power and His love for you.

Have you believed you've messed up so bad it almost "cripples" you? What I mean by cripple, you don't want to make new decisions, but that is unrealistic. You must unfreeze yourself. Your maker can help you get unstuck. Go forward remembering you survived. The honorable political leader Nelson Mandela was a South African anti-apartheid revolutionary and philanthropist who served as the first president of South Africa from 1994 to 1999. He is known for saying he never loses. He either wins or he learns.

Ponder on the life of Jacob's son Joseph. His story is found in the Bible's Book of Genesis. The Andrew Lloyd Webber and Tim Rice musical *Joseph and the Amazing Technicolor Dreamcoat* was based on his life. The legendary story is about a man who made the "mistake" of sharing his dream to his brothers that they bowed down to him and this led them to sell him into slavery. What looked like a tragic mistake ultimately led him to be king and he saved his country and family from a famine. The dream came to pass about 22 years later and Joseph did reign over his brothers. Was it a mistake that Joseph told his brothers the dream?

Move!

When picking beautiful roses, you can get pricked by thorns. There are times when something breaks and you can't put the pieces together, but you CAN use the pieces to move forward.

The Lord promises that He would complete that which he started (Philippians 1:6). Discover confidence in the Lord's promises. Furthermore, let him reveal the ram in the bushes.

God knows the end of your story. It has been said that when something breaks in life, we may not always be able to put it back together, but we can use those pieces to make something new.

Do think God didn't know you would do that? Let Him take over. No one can "mess up" too much that God can't use you or make the matter turn out for your good. He is the all-powerful God. Nothing is impossible for Him.

God can create incredible good out of unspeakable tragedies. He can help you orchestrate the necessary strategies to catapult you to your victory.

God is a good God. There is evil among us killing, stealing, and destroying (John 10:10).

Consider the Biblical heroes. Moses killed a man. The apostle Paul persecuted Christians before he became a prominent figure who played an influential role in introducing the gospel. Also, David arranged for the inevitable death of the man whose wife he desired.

"*Many are the plans in the mind of a man, but it is the purpose of the Lord that will stand.*" (Proverbs 19:21 ESV). God calls, He prepares, and gets us ready. Many are called, but few are chosen.

We are told in the Bible to, "*Count it all joy, my brothers, when you meet trials of various kinds, for you know that the testing of your faith produces steadfastness*" (James 1:2). Isaiah 61:3 speaks of how the Lord makes beauty out of our ashes.

Is what you did, or what someone did to you too impossible for God to "fix"? Nothing is too impossible for God (Genesis 18:14, Jeremiah 32:27; Luke 1:37). All things are possible with Him. The use of the word "fix" may not mean a return to the previous condition. "Fix" may refer to as restore, transform, reveal, and other endless possibilities.

If you would have done one thing differently, the outcome would be different. Trust God. The Holy Spirit is your hiding place.

Learn how to make lemonade out of every lemon experience. When my plane is delayed, I think of it as an extra hour to read or catch up on correspondences. Think...about all the *potential advantages* a problem might produce.

In Romans 12:2, the apostle Paul wrote,

> *"Do not be conformed to this world, but be transformed by the renewal of your mind, that by testing you may discern what is the will of God, what is good and acceptable and perfect".*

The believer is strengthened by the promises of God's guidance. Isn't there more than one way to do something? Find contentment in God's Will and plan for your life.

The Bible speaks of the "will of God" in various ways. The *permissible will of God* is referred to when the will of God is a topic is described as what God permits. This notion is not specifically mentioned in the Bible, but it is often described as what God allows in one's life.

The idea that God permits something does not mean it is His will, or not His will. Ponder on that notion.

The Lord is described in the Word as gentle and does not force anyone to do His will. He is recognized for allowing everyone the power to choose.

There is a theory that what is known as God's permissible will does not have His full blessings. If this theory is true, we can rely on His promise in Romans 8:28 that He promised that all things work together for a good for those who love the Lord.

I heard Bishop TD Jakes share during one of his sermons "what you call failure is correction". He went on to share how what you refer to as losing, you never had, but a substitute for the real thing. Jakes encourages people not to process the matter as a loss. The bishop also pointed out how God cares enough to help you get the process right and He loves you enough to confront your strong stubborn will so He can give you what He has for you.

Day by day we face windows of opportunities. The reference to a window helps us recognize we are to look through the glass and determine steps to take before we go through doors. As you gaze through life's windows, you can plan and prepare to execute with the tools you learn along the way.

God has a plan for us. Find peace in exploring your purpose and season in your life. Find your purpose and you find your peace. Your choices and path shape you for your purpose. Ultimately, living in your purpose helps you find peace in the paths that may have been bumpy along the way. One day we will reach the light at the end of the tunnel.

Find your purpose and you find your peace.

Life has turning points. The doors open for you to the path and purpose-designed for your life may not always be clear. Sometimes, we miss a door. Doors are not always open.

Some doors need keys, some open at certain times, some doors are permanent. You may need to be at a certain perimeter for a door to begin opening for you. If you walk through some doors, your life can change forever. Some doors are not God's will for you to enter and God closes them to protect you. God knows everything and He knows if you're on a path that leads to danger, or that is not aligned with the plan He has for you. Doesn't that sound like a loving Father?

Everything is beautiful in God's timing (Ecclesiastes 3:11). There is seasonal timing and cycles. Pray to be in step with His timing for you. Pray to know what to do in this time of your life. We know that the

Bible says all things work together for good to them that love God, to them who are the called according to *His* purpose (Romans 8:28).

Stand still and take time to review your life. Review, strategize and download from heaven to get direction. Receive answers and insight from our Father God. It is wise to allow the prompting of His Spirit to guide us.

Review, strategize and download from heaven to get direction.

Learning how to rest in God is a step in how to move forward effectively. Guidance from the Creator is important. He desires to spend time with us. Let Him call you into alignment. When one is not in alignment, they are not at ease and this could lease to disease. Be still and know He is God (Psalm 46:10).

Review	Strategize	Download

____

____

____

Chapter 5

What Did You Learn?

*"Learn from the mistakes of others.
You can't live long enough to make them all yourself."*

- Eleanor Roosevelt

You will make mistakes. Learn from each one. Experience a revelation. People grow. Seek insight. Nothing that happened will be wasted. The advice if you continue to carry the bricks from your past, you will end up building the same house is a reminder to learn from the past and proceed accordingly.

We must exercise the opportunity to reevaluate, regroup & revamp to avoid future apprehension. Ask yourself," What did I learn from this experience?" Begin to reevaluate, regroup, and revamp.

Reevaluate	**Regroup**	**Revamp**

What 3 things have influenced your life the most? For example: your faith, the way you look, or your decisions.

1. ____________________

2. ____________________

3. ____________________

Life is not like an exam or test in school that you failed or didn't do what you expected where you deliberate on and restudy to pass the retest. Of course, we reflect and consider how we could have done things differently, but there is no exact science when it comes to this type of reflection. There are so many factors to consider that may have influence an outcome. We don't always have specific answers to questions as an exam. The test key and answers of life may be more like essay questions with various possible responses.

It is necessary to be easy on ourselves. It is toxic to be bitter and resentful to anyone. This includes yourself. God wants us to forgive, let go and move on. This is healthier and freer. Balance is necessary. Meaning we must be responsible and thoughtful. Don't dump on yourself too hard. This may result in physical harm. When we break down the word disease, we find disease.

According to Merriam Webster Dictionary, the original use of the word *disease* was not a reference to an illness, but trouble, discomfort, uneasiness, distress. Webster's online dictionary shares in the 14th century, Oxford English Dictionary defined the term as the *lack of ease*. In addition, at the turn of the 16th century, *disease* was referred to as "a case of illness, or specific illnesses and maladies".

Ultimately, the prefix *dis* - suggests a lack of ease. The Webster's online dictionary also explained how the over 800-year history of *ease* is related to the state of being comfortable, including freedom from pain or discomfort. Be kind and gracious to yourself so you can enjoy life and avoid disEase.

Some people have been hard on themselves their entire life. If they didn't get straight A's in school or didn't perform well at work, they condemn themselves and find themselves using negative self-talk which may lead to other unwanted circumstances.

Life is not an exam. You can: try again, look at someone else's paper – it's not cheating, ask for help or start over.

The difference between your today and the future is information. If you don't learn anything new today, tomorrow will be just like your today. You don't want a long today, but a future. Listen, observe, gather information, and observe again. Your future is in your new discoveries if you allow it to be.

Listen, observe, gather information, and observe again.

I remember hearing a story about a young man in the hospital as a result of an injury that left him paralyzed. One day he began singing out loud "If I could do it all over again" over and over. An elderly patient overheard him and said, *"You would mess up all over again"*. Initially, that sounds funny, but it really isn't. It is interesting how people can make the same mistake, the same poor decisions, or the same poor choices over and over again. This suggests we must study the present moment.

People may experience the pain and often destruction of decisions of their past but find themselves in the circumstance again. Also, people may watch the errors of others and end up repeating the behavior. *How are lessons learned?*

Life can be a wonder. Some decisions leave us scratching our heads.

Why?
What happened?
What?
No way!

The award-winning record producer, musician, songwriter, composer, arranger, and tv producer, Quincy Jones, once said "You Make Your Mistakes to Learn How to Get to the Good Stuff".

Your previous decisions tell you about how you think, process information, how you feel, and what you need. They reveal a lot about you. “Listen” rather than frustrate yourself. Hone into each moment and grow.

Don’t mistake poor decisions with making a mistake, or human error. Could it be rash decisions, poor planning, or irresponsible behavior? Ask yourself questions…were you using good judgment?

When we take time to evaluate our thinking, we may learn how to navigate wisely next time. The discoveries we make can help us navigate effectively and less emotionally. Take time to explore and heal.

We develop good judgment over time. There are various components contributing to our judgment. As you evaluate, be sure to use ALL available information. Information is valuably powerful.

Age	**Information**	**Motive**
Wisdom	**Details**	**Guidance**
Insight	**Context**	**Perspective**

Decisions and choices all require strategy, as well as maturity. I teach my psychology students that problem-solving is a form of development.

Embracing *mistakes may* actually turn things around. Why wallow in self-pity when you can look for the silver lining? It is important to step back and take a look at our circumstances. Try to redefine the moment. Regroup when necessary. Explore the vantage points.

We have what I like to call our own personal rearview windows. These are tools available to us guiding us through decisions, but they do not always work effectively.

"They" say Hindsight is 20-20. People want 20-20 vision, but our rearview window may not be enough sometimes, or our blind spots hinder us.

Foresight is defined by Merriam Webster as an act of looking forward. After discoveries are made, we use new lenses.

Throughout my years of teaching, if a student makes a mistake in front of the class, it never fails, they tend not to make that mistake on the exam. This is particularly true if they made the mistake, and their classmates witnessed the error.

Some oops are painful, time-consuming, and draining. Some are actually funny or enlightening. Yes, funny. Laughing at ourselves may help lighten the moment and give a fresh perspective. Take a step back and look at the big picture.

We may miss the mark. Learning from errors helps make it all worth it. It's not over until God says it's over.

For years, I looked at my first moving violation ticket as so absurd. A police officer pulled me over because I didn't form a complete stop before turning right at a light. I couldn't confidently argue the point, because I truly couldn't recall if my stop was complete, or a slow turn. The incident has influenced my right turn on reds until this day. I haven't turned right on red the same. The experience impacted me long term. Moreover, it may have saved me from many more tickets, or car accidents. I trust God that random traffic stop during my first month of driving worked out for my good.

If we thought of life like a financial transaction, we would require a reduction of the cost for mistakes. Refunds for time wasted may be warranted. We should appraise the value of relationships while putting liabilities up for sale. Lastly, we would cash in promises. Sadly, this is not how things go. Although, the transactions may be costly, the process is not as cut and dry as financial transactions.

Tell yourself the truth. How do you feel about the circumstance, disappointment, pain, or mistake? This will initiate the ability to foster change and healthier thinking. This step may help you think clearer to process the matter effectively. Moreover, you may discover what you did may be exactly something you should have done, you won.

Although, you may appear to be winning don't outrun your faith or reliance on God! Faith and presumption are often a matter confused and could give "stepping out on faith" a bad name. Learn to have the Lord lead you. Lean on God. The author and finisher of our faith (Hebrews 12:2).

Let's follow the Lord's instructions to pray without ceasing. In the Bible's 1 Thessalonians 5:16-18, we are instructed to

Rejoice always, pray without ceasing,

give thanks in all circumstances;

for this is the will of God

in Christ Jesus for you.

Praying without ceasing isn't merely clasping our hands and closing our eyes while bringing our petitions to God 24/7. It is the continual communication and acknowledgement of the heavenly Father throughout our day. Checking in, run something by, sharing gratitude, enjoying His presence, and communing with Him is all a part of praying without ceasing. Ultimately, we seek His wisdom and guidance to navigate through life.

Wisdom is the principal thing according to Proverbs 4:7. *What is wisdom?* The ability to discern the difference is impactful. Discerning the difference between right and wrong, or a moment in time may also be impactful.

Discerning the difference in people who should be in our lives also requires wisdom and at times difficult discissions. Who belongs in your life and who no longer belongs in your life?

IN? ______________________________

OUT? ______________________________

IN? ______________________________

OUT? ______________________________

In our confusion, darkness, and testing, we discover the truth about ourselves, others and about our Creator. We may even find that our testing leads to a deeper trust and relationship with Him.

Try this prayer in those moments of uncertainty.

God, I don't know if what I'm experiencing is
you're testing me or not, but either way,
I want to trust You.
I give my future to you.
Amen

Looking back can be costly. Reduce the size of your rear-view window. While walking forward, if you look back you may trip or turn into salt.

In Genesis 19, Lot was warned that the land was to be destroyed and to leave immediately when two angels in the form of men approached him. After much hesitation and his home being physically confronted by the men of Sodom seeking the angels, Lot and his family finally made the move to escape.

They were given specific instructions in verse 17 *"Don't look back, and don't stop anywhere in the plain!"* While in route out of the city, Lot's wife looked back at the destruction, against the angels' instruction. As a consequence, she turned into a pillar of salt.

Lot's wife was a native of Sodom which would explain her longing for the area and the people, which may have caused her to turn back to see its destruction. Then she turned into a pillar of salt. There were lessons in Lot and his wife's story. Mourning the loss of what is familiar may be very costly. Also, not following directions may cost us our lives.

If you didn't learn the lesson the first time, thank God you are still here to have another chance to get it RIGHT. No Condemnation, but this is your life. You may need to regroup or seek reinforcements to help get you on the right track.

I used to run track. During the relay races, I loved the pressure of being the last person to bring it home. Sometimes life is like a relay race, and you need help from a team to bring home the win.

If you keep finding yourself on the same wrong road or dead end, there may be a reason why. If you keep making the same mistakes it might be time to get help from prayer, pastoral guidance, counseling, therapy, coaching, support groups, or self-help tools to find out why. Get answers!

Proverbs 11:14 shares *Where no counsel is, the people fall: but in the multitude of counselors, there is safety.* Seek professional wisdom, help and assistance.

The Bible demonstrates how intentional and strategic God is. We too should strive to make intentional and strategic decisions in our lives. Counting the cost of decisions may save us from a lifetime of pain and disappointment.

It is time for me to announce God doesn't bring evil, nor illness to our lives, but allows it…*to turn around and use for a good* (Romans 8:28). Although, it is important to be mindful there is an adversary looking to destroy lives (1 Peter 5:8).

Learning to bypass traps and snares is a useful tool. God demonstrates this all throughout the Bible. God doesn't create the storms but permits them for various reasons as not breaking His own laws, or His Word (the Bible) to offer teachable moments. When the Lord delivers you from circumstances, it will give Him glory and bring people to Him.

What has the Lord delivered you from?

Your testimony can set people FREE.

Your testimony can set people free. It is your unique story that can help encourage and lift up others. People love stories. We watch movies, tv and read stories.

Your testimony can inspire and offer experiences to emulate. Your story can show people they are not alone. Glorify the goodness of the Lord with your testimony.

As our Lord teaches us through the storms of life and turning points, we learn about His goodness. He demonstrates His power while exercising our dependence on Him.

We learn to trust God through storms.

We learn to trust God through storms. Trusting Him will strengthen our faith. The opposite of faith is fear, but the wrong fear. We are taught to fear God with astonishing reverence. Not fear that is a result of lack of faith, but fear as to revere, respect and hold in highest regard.

In the book of 1st Kings, the prophet Elijah was described to experience fear and even dismay. A prophet is defined by the Merriam Webster Dictionary as one who utters divinely inspired revelations: such as the writers of the prophetic books of the Bible. The dictionary also mentions the term is referred to one who is regarded by a group of followers as the final authoritative revealer of God's will.

Accounts of Elijah in the Bible's book of 1st Kings, describes him as a man who walked with and heard from God. Although, he experienced great disappointment in himself and others. Also, despite his reputation of great faith, he was afraid. Genesis 5:24 gives record of Elijah being taken directly to heaven without dying. His fear and dismay never found him. Fortunately, sometimes the thing someone is running from may never find them.

Trust

A lack of trust can lead to depression and fear. Fear can lead to violence, depression, and oppressing others. Ultimately, fear is destructive and hinders our peace. It is important not to allow fear to take over. We want and need peace!

Developing trust in God and the life He gave us, will helps us understanding challenging moments and give us the strength we need to carry us through. Life will have hard times. Every experience builds faith and the trust needed.

Don't ever think when you don't understand a matter, or don't "hear" an answer from God, He isn't with you, or listening. In Hebrews 13:5 Jesus said, "I will never leave you nor forsake you". God is all-knowing and omnipresent. Matthew 28:20 tells us He is with us always, even to the end. When you get to know a person, you start to trust or understand them. Get to know your Father God.

In the book of Psalms in chapter 138 versus 7 and 8. We read of how though we may walk in troubled times, God will stretch out his hands to protect us while working out His plans for our lives. The Lord promises never to abandon us.

The Word of God instructs us to seek God's will in all we do, and He will show us which path to take. We are not to be wise in our own eyes but fear the Lord and refuse to do wrong (Proverbs 3:6-7). God is with us and bringing us through. Building your life on that truth helps us trust the path.

It is best to forget the *mistake* and remember the lesson. "To change the past is a big order, but you can change the future," said Timon, the meerkat from Lion King story.

The expression *what will be will be* is used to describe the notion that fate will decide the outcome of a course of events, even if action is taken to try to alter it. "Que Sera, Sera (Whatever Will Be, Will Be)" is a popular song written by the team of Jay Livingston and Ray Evans that was first published in 1955.

Doris Day sang the song in the Alfred Hitchcock film The Man Who Knew Too Much (1956). The song has been recorded dozens of times by dozens of singers. Ponder on the words of the song on the next page.

QUE SERA, SERA
(WHATEVER WILL BE, WILL BE)

When I was just a little girl
I asked my mother, what will I be
Will I be pretty, will I be rich
Here's what she said to me

Que sera, sera
Whatever will be, will be
The future's not ours to see
Que sera, sera
What will be, will be

When I grew up and I fell in love
I asked my sweetheart what lies ahead
Will we have rainbows day after day
Here's what my sweetheart said

Que sera, sera
Whatever will be, will be
The future's not ours to see
Que sera, sera
What will be, will be

Now I have children of my own
They ask their mother, what will I be
Will I be handsome, will I be rich
I tell them tenderly

Que sera, sera
Whatever will be, will be
The future's not ours to see
Que sera, sera
What will be, will be
Que sera, sera

Chapter 6

Forgive Yourself: Set yourself free.

"To err is human; to forgive, divine." Alexander Pope

Ponder on the following warnings.

Don't lose your childhood yearning to be an adult.

Don't let your 20s fly by while you look back at disappointments in your childhood.

Don't let your 30s get caught up in working too hard to be the person you wanted to be in your 20s.

Don't let your 40s get tripped up because of actions in your 20s and 30s you regret.

Don't spend your 50s sick because you weren't health conscious in your early years.

Don't spend your 60s in fear that you may not make it to 100.

Don't spend your 70s stressing over everyone else's pain in their young years.

Don't get lost in the physical pain of your 80s.

Don't miss out on your golden 90s trying to remember yesterday. Live today!

We do not have the luxury to press rewind. Disappointments and *mistakes* may be painful. Guilt can strangle people. Is it time for you to acknowledge, accept, and embrace everything about you?

There is wisdom in forgiving the past and responsibly moving forward. Scars can run deep. Some scars are self-inflicted. They may be due to mishandling of life. When you allow yourself to recognize you survived and actually came out better after the fall, you allow yourself to fully heal.

Not forgiving yourself may causes you to make mistakes over and over again. Unforgiveness ties you up.

Don't wallow in a whirlwind of regrets, or what could have happened. You survived!

The fog of regrets keeps you from looking at the light at the end of the tunnel. If you are alive to read this book, no matter how many mistakes you made, you can always make other choices while you have breath. You are alive. Live!

The fog of regrets keeps you from looking at the light at the end of the tunnel.

God's grace is sufficient for you. *Have you asked God to fix" it"?* What parent wouldn't help their child who made a mistake? Well, I suppose there are some parents who may want to see their child suffer after making a mistake, but not our merciful and gracious God!

Do you know God loves you? Nothing can separate you from the love of God (Romans 8:38). The Father's love is never-ending. The song Jesus Loves me says it all…

Jesus Loves me this I know. For the Bible tells me so. Little one to Him belong. They are weak, but He is strong. Yes, Jesus loves me. Yes, Jesus loves me. Yes, Jesus loves me. For the Bible tells me so.

When we read 1 Corinthians 13:4-8 we find...

Love is patient and kind; love does not envy or boast; it is not arrogant or rude. It does not insist on its own way; it is not irritable or resentful; it does not rejoice at wrongdoing but rejoices with the truth. Love bears all things, believes all things, hopes all things, endures all things.

Obsessing over what if's is senseless. One by one, look back at your what if's. Come up with a list of why you should be grateful for the outcomes. Also, consider the power and freedom in praising God because you are "okay". It is astonishing to see how things worked out and even worked out for good.

All those mishaps led you to where you are today. This could be good, bad, or an opportunity. Wrong roads have led people to life-changing circumstances.

You wish you didn't meet him or her, but why not find peace in you met him or her. Your life wouldn't be the same if you did or didn't. Your story would be altered. The world would be different without that chapter in the story.

People letting us down may be painful. Letting ourselves down may also be painful. Why add to the pain, awkwardness, and possible shame, by adding condemnation? Expecting people to do what you would do in a situation opens you up for disappointment. This also includes yourself. When you disappoint yourself, also remember to be conscious if you are exercising realistic expectations of yourself.

Forgive the decision-making skills of the 19-year-old you.

With age and maturity, we acquire skills equipping us with the ability to make better decisions. Forgive the decision-making skills of the 19-year-old you. Give yourself permission to receive the free gift of forgiveness.

Ask for grace, mercy, and for God to change His mind. This is one of the wonders of Christianity. Does God, the Creator and the almighty change His mind? Yes, change His mind. Apparently, in the Bible there is evidence that He has changed His mind, but when does He do it, and why does He do it is the mystery.

The Lord says in Jeremiah 26:3…

Perhaps they will listen and each
one will turn back from his evil way,
and I will change my mind concerning
the calamity that I intend to bring on
them because of their evil deeds.

All things are possible with God. (Matthew 19:26)

Can prayer or supplications change our course? It's a mystery, but nevertheless, God's Will be done. Thank God not all our prayers were answered.

If God will move on behalf of those who have done evil, how much more will He do for those who serve Him? All things are possible with God (Matthew 19:26).

You can NEVER mess up to the point of no return while you are still alive. If you have been misguided, on the wrong track, or off track. Let God reroute you. You are His creation. Someone else's life may never be complete without you.

Philippians 4:8 shares...

Finally, brethren, whatsoever things
aretrue, whatsoever things are honest,
whatsoever things are just,
whatsoever things are pure,
whatsoever things are lovely,
whatsoever things are of good report;
if there be any virtue,
and if there be any praise,
think on these things.

The late Pastor Henry Wright of Be in Health Ministries' research reveals there are health concerns rooted in resentment, self-condemnation, and bitterness. His ministry researches the root causes of diseases and presents an understanding of human physiology.

Proverbs 17:22 explains how "a merry heart doeth good *like* medicine: but a broken spirit drieth the bones." Pray God heals your heart so you may maintain a merry heart. There is refuge and restoration in the hands of our heavenly Father.

This and other similar teachings encourage us to resist thoughts of fear, guilt, shame, and even accusation towards oneself, or God because it results in disease.

In addition, thoughts of hate, self-hatred, rejection, and fear are also toxic and interfere with our identity. This path prevents us from reaching our full potential of who we are created to be.

One day you will reach the point when you praise God and thank Him for your journey. Yes! Thank Him.

Contentment is a wise desire. Your so-called mistakes don't define you. It is what you do after that counts. Can you find comfort in the words of Acts 3:19 that after the error, turn to God, so He can wipe it out, and there will be a time of refreshing from the Lord?

Discover your true meaning and transform your life.

How are you measuring your life? Find your true element. Discover your true meaning and transform your life.

Give up the notion that the past could have been different!

Free yourself from old narratives. Free yourself from your past so you can enjoy the present that you were created for. It's in the past where it belongs. Give up the notion that the past could have been different! God forgives you. Forgive yourself. Let it be well with your soul.

Read the lyrics of the Beatles song *Let It Be* on the next few pages. The words express life's journey.

Let It Be

When I find myself in times of trouble, Mother Mary
comes to me
Speaking words of wisdom, let it be and in my hour of darkness,
She is standing right in front of me speaking words of wisdom,
let it be
Let it be, let it be, let it be, let it be
Whisper words of wisdom, let it be
And when the broken-hearted people living in the world agree
There will be an answer, let it be for though
they may be parted,
there is still a chance that they will see
there will be an answer, let it be
Let it be, let it be, let it be, let it be
There will be an answer, let it be

Let it be, let it be, let it be, let it be

Whisper words of wisdom, let it be

Let it be, let it be, let it be, let it be

Whisper words of wisdom, let it be, and when the night is cloudy

There is still a light that shines on me

Shinin' until tomorrow, let it be

I wake up to the sound of music, Mother Mary comes to me

Speaking words of wisdom, let it be

And let it be, let it be, let it be, let it be

Whisper words of wisdom, let it be

And let it be, let it be, let it be, let it be

Whisper words of wisdom, let it be

Chapter 7

Now what? Prepare for next time. There will be a next time.

"For I know the plans *and* thoughts that I have for you", says the LORD, "plans for peace *and* well-being and not for disaster, to give you a future and a hope".
Jeremiah 29:11 Amplified Bible (AMP)

"I know what I am planning for you", says the Lord, "I have good plans for you, not plans to hurt you. I will give you hope and a good future".
Jeremiah 29:11 New Century Version

No one can turn back the hands of time, but God. How He does it is His Will. The way the Lord God addresses the plan for our lives is sovereign. Although, this is contingent on us seeking Him and serving Him.

When someone is lost or has lost their way, they may be in the wilderness looking for a path out. God and His wisdom are the paths out.

As God watches people parade around, He knows the plan He has for us. It is so clear in story after story in the Bible. Consider the stories of Sampson, Joseph, the Blessed Mother Mary, Abraham, Moses, Isaac, Jacob, and Jesus. God has a plan for us!

Now what? What do you do next time? Where do you go from here? Embrace change! In each moment of our lives, we are creating the story of our life. Make it a great day! I remember when I heard that for the first time. It was an “ah-ha” moment. When I first heard that statement, a young person, my daughter’s teenage friend said it. It changed my life. It rang in my mind, heart, and soul like a charge. We seize our moment and moments.

Embrace moments calmly to discover the mystery in each moment. Don’t get caught in the sticky moments and block yourself from seeing possibilities and hidden treasures. Don’t forget to applaud yourself when you do well.

We make our day great. Make it a great day. Let God's infinite wisdom take you from day to day through prayer, meditating on His Words in the Bible, trusting in Him, and exercising faith in Him.

In 1988 Bobby McFerrin came out with a song called "Don't Worry Be Happy". The internationally hit song held the number-one position on the Billboard magazine Hot 100 chart for 2 weeks. The song opens with:

"Don't Worry Be Happy"

Here's a little song I wrote
You might want to sing it note for note
Don't worry, be happy
In every life we have some trouble
But when you worry you make it double
Don't worry, be happy
Don't worry, be happy now

By now I hope you realized it is important to observe our perspective of "mistakes". If not, now you know. We have experiences. What we do with those experiences and how we react to them make a world of difference.

No, I am not suggesting making excuses for bad behavior, or irresponsible living. I'm suggesting strongly to move forward with wisdom and clarity, not fear and dismay.

Walk tall. Learn from others' experiences and your personal experiences. Walk with big ears listening to the guidance of the Holy Spirit that dwells in you. The Holy Spirit is your comforter. When fearful, read the Psalms. I once read, "Those who walk with God always reach their destination."

Practice the presence of God and meditate on the scripture to hear from God. Receiving guidance from God requires getting to know His voice. Reading the Bible, praying, praising Him and merely sitting in His presence during quite moments all aide in our skill to hear the voice of God,

Discernment is also a necessary skill, or some may call a gift to ask God for and develop. It is defined as the ability to notice the intricate details, the ability to judge something well, or the ability to understand and comprehend something. A good example of discernment is one's observation of the particular details in a painting and understanding what makes the art good and bad.

Asking yourself the right questions and assessing matters accordingly is required when utilizing discernment. Define relevant moments and compare appropriate examples of standards as part of the process.

The questionable sixth sense, commonly referred to as a woman's intuition, and so-called psychic powers are ideas related to insight helping guide decisions. They are just that- ideas or possibilities.

These options may open opportunities for deception. Deception can make people go down the wrong path. Demonic influence may deceive people to turn and twist their thinking to make them think they are doing the right thing. Before you doubt demonic activity, consider external influences that deceive, mislead, or confuse people's thinking.

There is a way *that seems* right to a man, but its end *is* the way of death (Proverbs 14:12). We have an adversary wishing us no good. It is necessary to be cautious and seek Godly wisdom.

In John 10:10, the Bible refers to…The thief does not come except to steal, and to kill, and to destroy. I have come that they may have life and that they may have *it* more abundantly.

Being mindful that we are in a war is wise. We must be on the watch to protect our lives. God is with us always to help guide us in the correct direction. In the book of John chapter 10 verse 27, the Lord says his sheep hear His voice, and "I know them, and they follow Me". Are you his sheep? Are you His? Are you spending time with your Creator to get to know His voice? Each turn in life, and each experience helps us discern the Lord's voice.

According to Deuteronomy 31:6, we are to be strong and of good courage, do not fear nor be afraid; for the LORD your God, He *is* the One who goes with you. He will not leave you nor forsake you. More specifically, your spirit is the candle of God, and will guide you (Proverbs 20:27).

It is not over yet. You have time. You have time to make a difference, turn things around, or seek an opportunity to make sense of matters. If you have breath and life, you have time. Use it wisely.

Weeping may endure for a night, but joy cometh in the morning (Psalm 30:5). Breathe. Count to 10. Cry if necessary. Then, start coming up with a game plan. Ask God, “What is next”!?!?

Are you obsessing over a decision you made? Stop worrying or obsessing but start living. You have breath, you survived, so you have hope. Take the challenge to do better, get better, and live smarter.

Do Better	**Get Better**	**Live Smatter**

Seek divine guidance during your glorious destiny. There are 800,000 Words in the Bible, it takes 56 hours to read it through. Read the Bible daily. One recommendation is to read a Proverb a day. Enjoy exploring and discovering answers.

The Bible is known to be pregnant with revelation. You may read the same verse multiple times and receive a different understanding or message that is timely for your current situation. Each verse may uncover truth and bring things to light for you.

Pray for supernatural revelation of who God is and His plans for your life. Under the guidance of His Spirit, you can experience revelation. This level of communication may give birth to great understanding. Psalms 37:23 *tells us the steps of a good man are ordered by the Lord.*

Also, seek the Lord's Grace. Grace is God's unmerited favor. God is for us. If He is for us, who can be against us (Romans 8:31)?

God reminds us of His love daily and helps us see that we are wonderfully and fearfully made (*Psalm 139:13-14)*. Walk confidently in your greatness. Don't deny yourself of your destiny.

Pray for wisdom and God's grace that even your mistakes work out for good because you love the Lord

(Romans 8:28). Ask yourself what have you learned? What can you avoid next time?

Time is interesting. Things truly change with time. We grow and develop. If you have time, you have life. If you have life, you have an opportunity for change. Possibilities are endless.

No, we don't have the luxury to press rewind in life or call for a do-over. Although, we can live today so we don't say we want a do-over in 10 years.

We do have time to make new choices and learn more options. Moreover, taking time to identify why one's path led down a particular journey is a valuable experience.

Psalm 37:31 in the Contemporary English Version of the Bible shares *Those who remember God's teachings, will never take a wrong step.* The English Revised Version of this text explains this holds true because the law of his God is in his heart. This passage isn't suggesting we won't make errors, but the suggestion is what we are calling an error may be part of God's plan for our lives. Ultimately, the plan God has for us is to bring us to true fulfillment.

We don't have a "life pencil" with an eraser on it, but we do have the option to change the *F* to an *E.* I'm a pro at fixing mistakes on greeting cards by turning an error into a flower or a drawing. Now all the people who received cards from me and saw a random flower or drawing know why.

It is important to be diligent. There are consequences to decisions. Good decisions have good consequences. Not-so-good decisions have not-so-good consequences. Don't let one bad decision define the rest of your life.

Think "God-like" thoughts about you, your life, and possibilities. Bottom line, trust in the Lord. Trust God to transform you.

Have the blessed assurance that Jesus is yours. He is a fortress. We are overcomers.

Talk, walk and experience the victory. Shoot the next basket. This time it may go in. Don't take your ball and go home crying while hiding under your bed. Don't give up and sit on your couch eating bonbons or watching Tyler Perry movies.

Get back on that horse and try again. The next time may be the jackpot. No matter how you try, you can't fix everything, but you may fix something.

God's timing may not be our timing. If you are alive, you have time. Use it wisely.

Let us hold on to the guidance in Psalm 25:12 teaching us *"Those who have reverence for the LORD will learn from Him the path they should follow."*

Choose the Lord. Choose life. Trust the process. Trust yourself. Trust God. The Word of God explains in Proverbs 3:5 that we should…

Trust in the LORD with all your heart
and lean not on your own understanding.
In all your ways acknowledge Him, and
He shall direct your paths.

Now would you change anything about your past? I wouldn't, and we can't.

I don't know what made you read this book, but I hope you found it and will use your *"life pencil eraser"*. Enjoy life!

The End.

Appendix

Dr. Soyini Richards' Theory

Be careful not to let the former years negatively impact the years you have ahead.

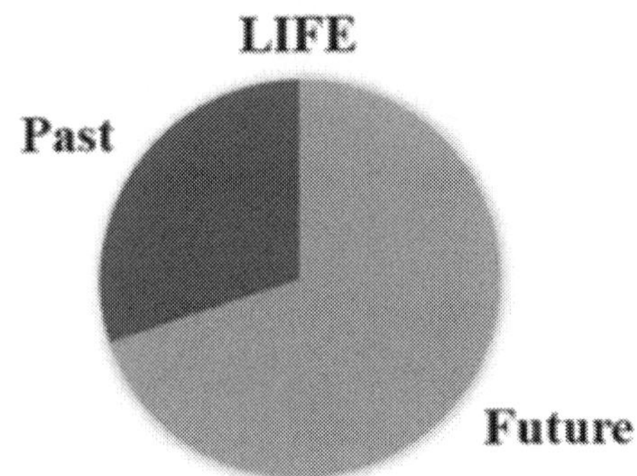

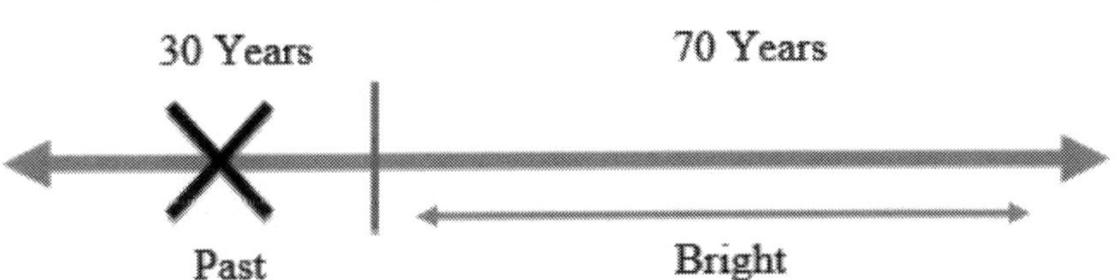

DECISION TREE EXAMPLE

DECISION TREE

DECISION TREE

References, Referrals & Resources

https://www.merriam-webster.com/

https://www.Biblehub.com

https://www.brainyquote.com/topics/making_mistakes

Be in Health Ministries
https://www.beinhealth.com/

Mike Murdock https://www.thewisdomcenter.tv/

Cindy Trim https://cindytrimmministries.org/

Bishop TD Jakes https://www.tdjakes.org/

Oprah Winfrey https://youtu.be/kfLGR0KYuys

Book- *Command Your Morning*, by Cindy Trimm
https://cindytrimmministries.org/power-up-your-day/

Tversky, A., & Kahneman, D. (1974). Judgment under uncertainty: Heuristics and biases. *Science, 185*(4157), 1124 - 1131.
https://doi.org/10.1126/science.185.4157.1124

Affirmations / Confessions

I am looking forward to an awesome future.
I do not make mistakes.
I make wise decisions.
I do not have regrets.
I do not have fears.
I have hope.
I am happy.
I am excited about life.
I am ready for a bright future.
I am getting better and better each day.
I made it.
I am worthy.
I am grateful.
I am at peace.
All is well.

Have you said this prayer before?

Dear God,

I come to You in the Name of Jesus.
I admit that I am not right with You, and
I want to be right with You.
I ask You to forgive me of all my sins.
The Bible says if I confess with my mouth that
"Jesus is Lord," and believe in my heart that God raised
Him from the dead, I will be saved (Rom. 10:9).
I believe with my heart, and I confess with my mouth that
Jesus is the Lord and Savior of my life.
Thank You for saving me!
In Jesus' name I pray.

Amen.

About the Author—

Dr. Soyini Ayanna Richards is a woman of God, author, business psychologist, therapeutic coach, school psychologist, and professor. Dr. Richards has a bachelor's in Psychology, master's in Counseling Psychology, and Ph.D. in Business Psychology. The native New Yorker is currently residing in the Washington, DC area. She attended Howard University for undergraduate and graduate school.

Dr. Richards had a thriving Christian psychotherapy practice in her hometown in Westchester, NY, where she offered individual and family therapy. Since the late 90's, Soyini Richards has worked in higher education as both a professor and an administrator. Professor Richards' taught at Spelman College, Georgetown University and other fine institutions across the US.

As a business psychologist and serial entrepreneur, Dr. Soyini Richards offers an array of services. She is practicing her two loves, psychology and business with excellence. Dr. Richards offers mental health coaching to businesses, government agencies, individuals, couples, youth and families. She is also the co-owner of Wellness Bliss offering an array of wellness services to the community. Her newest venture is Teachers Festival, Inc. celebrating and honoring educators worldwide.

The professor is known to inspire, motivate and transform lives. She teaches, talks to live audiences, and coaches people of all ages. Dr. Richards has noteworthy success with youth, college students, women, leaders and all while exercising Biblical principles. Professor Richards enjoys using her gifts from God to help people identify their callings and discover their true paths.

Dr. Richards has an extensive, as well as impressive network of friends and colleagues. She enjoys collaborating with others to reach the community. The professor participates in private and public events delivering empowering messages.

This proud mother and grandmother is dedicated to leave a legacy for many generations to come. Dr. Richards enjoys sharing with clients her age defying keys and her timeless jewels to enjoy life. She believes possibilities are endless.

*How to Fix Mistakes 101 i*s in Professor Richards' 101 Series of Books. Visit www.DrSoyini.com or email info@drsoyini.com for more information about the author and her services.

info@DrSoyini.com

www.DrSoyini.com

Made in the USA
Middletown, DE
27 October 2023